A Let's-Read-and-Find-Out Book™

COMETS

by Franklyn M. Branley   illustrated by Giulio Maestro

UPDATED EDITION

A Harper Trophy Book
Harper & Row, Publishers

The *Let's-Read-and-Find-Out Book*™ series was originated by Dr. Franklyn M. Branley, Astronomer Emeritus and former Chairman of the American Museum–Hayden Planetarium, and was formerly co-edited by him and Dr. Roma Gans, Professor Emeritus of Childhood Education, Teachers College, Columbia University. Text and illustrations for each of the more than 100 books in the series are checked for accuracy by an expert in the relevant field. The titles available in paperback are listed below. Look for them at your local bookstore or library.

Air Is All Around You
A Baby Starts to Grow
The BASIC Book
Bees and Beelines
Bits and Bytes
Comets
Corn Is Maize
Digging Up Dinosaurs
Dinosaurs Are Different
A Drop of Blood
Ducks Don't Get Wet
Fireflies in the Night
Flash, Crash, Rumble, and Roll
Fossils Tell of Long Ago
Germs Make Me Sick!
Gravity Is a Mystery

Hear Your Heart
How a Seed Grows
How Many Teeth?
How to Talk to Your Computer
Hurricane Watch
Is There Life in Outer Space?
Look at Your Eyes
Me and My Family Tree
Meet the Computer
The Moon Seems to Change
My Five Senses
My Visit to the Dinosaurs
No Measles, No Mumps for Me
Oxygen Keeps You Alive
The Planets in Our Solar System
Rock Collecting
Rockets and Satellites

The Skeleton Inside You
The Sky Is Full of Stars
Snow Is Falling
Straight Hair, Curly Hair
Sunshine Makes the Seasons
A Tree Is a Plant
Turtle Talk
Volcanoes
Water for Dinosaurs and You
What Happens to a Hamburger
What I Like About Toads
What Makes Day and Night
What the Moon Is Like
Why Frogs Are Wet
Wild and Woolly Mammoths
Your Skin and Mine

Comets

Text copyright © 1984 by Franklyn M. Branley
Illustrations copyright © 1984 by Giulio Maestro

Designed by Al Cetta

Published in hardcover by Thomas Y. Crowell, New York
First Harper Trophy edition, 1985.

Library of Congress Cataloging in Publication Data
Branley, Franklyn Mansfield, 1915–

   Comets.

   (Let's-read-and-find-out science book)
   Summary: Explains what comets are, how they are formed, and how their unusual orbits bring them into earth's view at predictable intervals, with a special focus on Halley's comet.
   1. Comets—Juvenile literature. 2. Halley's comet—Juvenile literature. [1. Comets. 2. Halley's comet] I. Maestro, Giulio, ill. II. Title. III. Series.
QB721.5.B73 1984   523.6   83-46161
ISBN 0-690-04414-3
ISBN 0-690-04415-1 (lib. bdg.)
  (A Harper trophy book)
  (Let's-read-and-find-out books)
ISBN 0-06-445017-1   85-42739

Updated Edition, 1987

Comets are parts of our solar system. Like the planets, they go around the sun.

Gas and dust tail

But comets are not made of solid rock like planets.
A comet is a ball of dust, stones and ice. Many
people call comets dirty snowballs.

The "snowball" may be only a few miles across. But when the sun heats this "snowball" much of it is changed to gases. The gases expand and form the comet's head, which may be thousands of miles across.

A comet may also have a tail, made of gases and dust. It can be millions of miles long.

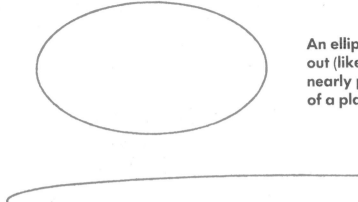

An ellipse can be flat and stretched out (like the orbit of a comet), or a nearly perfect circle (like the orbit of a planet).

Comets go around the sun. But they do not go around in circles. The path, or orbit, of a comet is a flattened circle—like the shape of a beach ball when you sit on it.

The shape of the orbit is called an ellipse. The sun is near one end of the ellipse. So during part of its journey a comet moves close to the sun. Most of the time, though, it is far away.

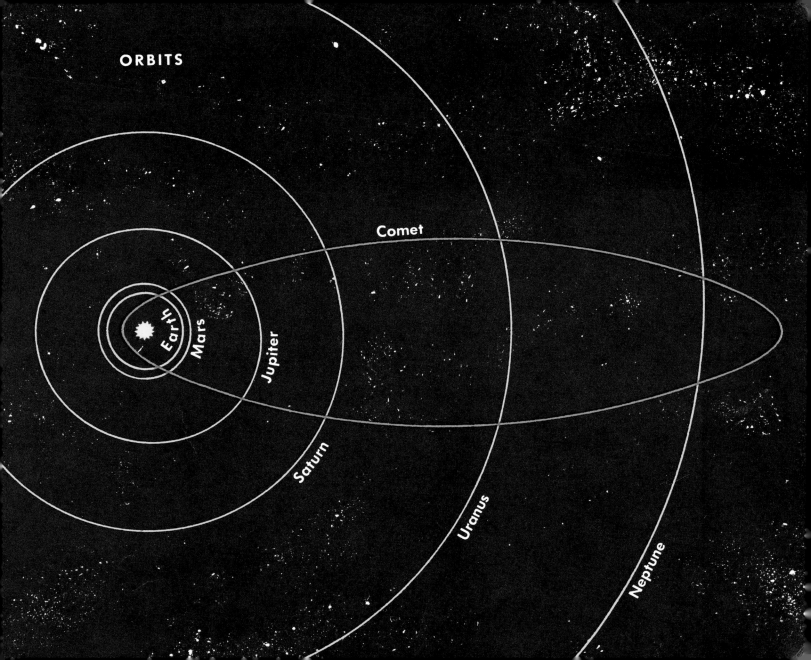

When a comet gets close to the sun, some of its dust and gases are pushed away from its head. The dust and gases stream away into space like hair. They make the comet's tail. People used to call comets "long-haired stars."

The sun gives off light—that we know. But it also throws off parts of itself—parts that are smaller than atoms. It is these particles that push the dust and gases away from the head of a comet. That's why the tail always points away from the sun.

When the comet is moving toward the sun, the tail is behind the head.

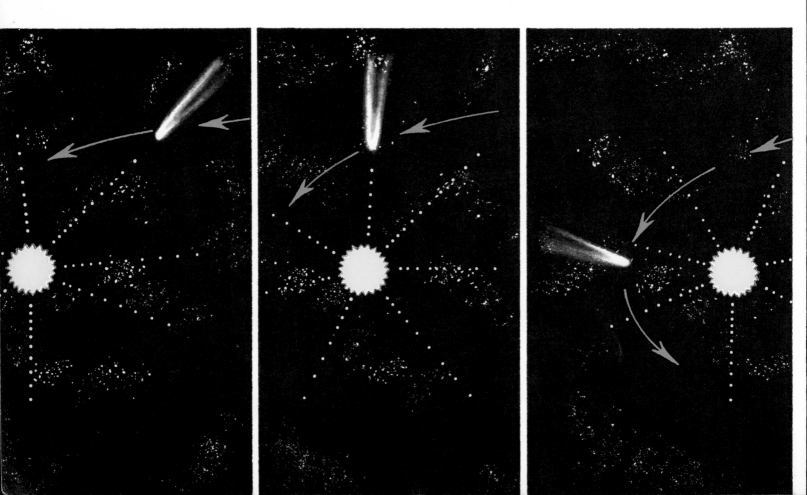

When the comet moves away from the sun, the tail
is in front of the head. But it is still called a tail.

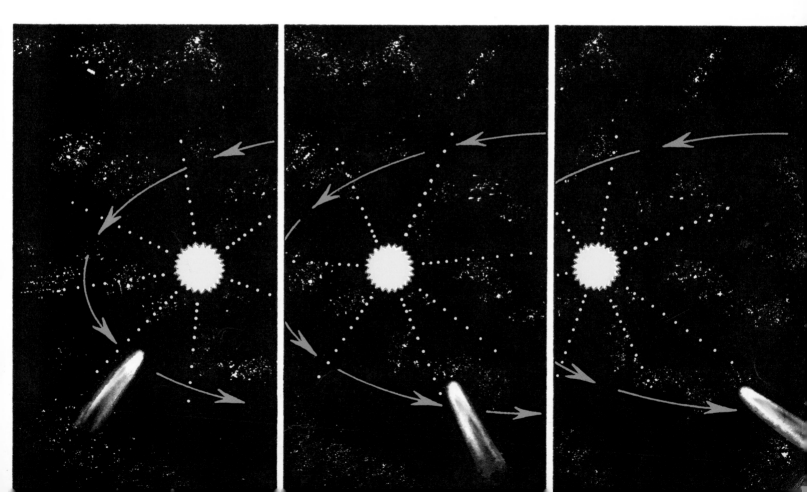

A comet moves fast in its trip around the sun. But when we see it, the comet does not seem to move. That's because it is so far away. The moon moves fast, but when you look at it, you can't see any motion. That's because the moon is far away.

So comets do not streak across the sky. You cannot see any motion. But if you look night after night, you can see that a comet changes position among the stars. If you watch the moon night after night, you'll see that it also changes position.

New comets appear every now and then. Also, "old" comets return. One is called Encke, after Johann F. Encke, the man who discovered that this comet returns every three years and four months. It is dim, so you need a telescope to see it.

Halley's comet, the most famous of all, returns every 76 years. Perhaps you saw it in December 1985, or in early 1986. You could see no tail unless you used binoculars. It looked like a dim, fuzzy star.

In 1986 spacecraft from the United States, Russia, Japan, and the European Space Agency moved close to Halley's comet. They found that the particles of gas and dust in the tail are as wispy as smoke from a wood fire. They can be seen when sunlight reflects from them.

The comet is made of carbon, nitrogen, oxygen, and stony dust, among other materials.

The center, or core, of the comet is a black, rocky lump, and it is not round. It is shaped somewhat like a potato, about six miles across at its longest part. The core rotates—it turns around once in about two days.

This picture of Halley's comet was made in 1986 using a large telescope-camera. It took 5 minutes to take the picture. You can see many streamers in the tail.

To an observer without a telescope, Halley would have looked like a dim, fuzzy star.

photo by Akira Fujii

For maybe 3000 years, or even a lot longer, Halley has been in orbit. About every 76 years it goes around the sun and then far out beyond Jupiter before making a return trip. When Halley is close to the sun, people can see it. They see it about every 76 years.

We hope you saw it in 1986. Julius Caesar, the Roman general, saw it in 87 B.C., when he was 13 years old.

People saw it in 1835 when Mark Twain was born. He was the man who wrote *Tom Sawyer*. The comet appeared again in 1910; that's when Mark Twain died.

Edmund Halley, an English astronomer, saw the comet in 1682. He discovered that the comet moves around the sun in an orbit shaped like an ellipse.

He also said it would return 76 years later. And it did. That's why the comet is named after him. Before Halley told them, people thought comets just wandered around the sky.

Halley lived about 300 years ago. In those days many people were afraid of comets. They thought a comet was a warning of something terrible that would soon occur. There might be a war, or a flood, or a famine. Perhaps there would be an earthquake. Others thought comets spread poison gases around the earth.

Comets were called disasters. The word "disaster" means evil star: *dis* means evil, and *aster* means star.

Comets are visitors that we see every once in a while. So they are exciting. But we know that comets cannot make terrible things happen.

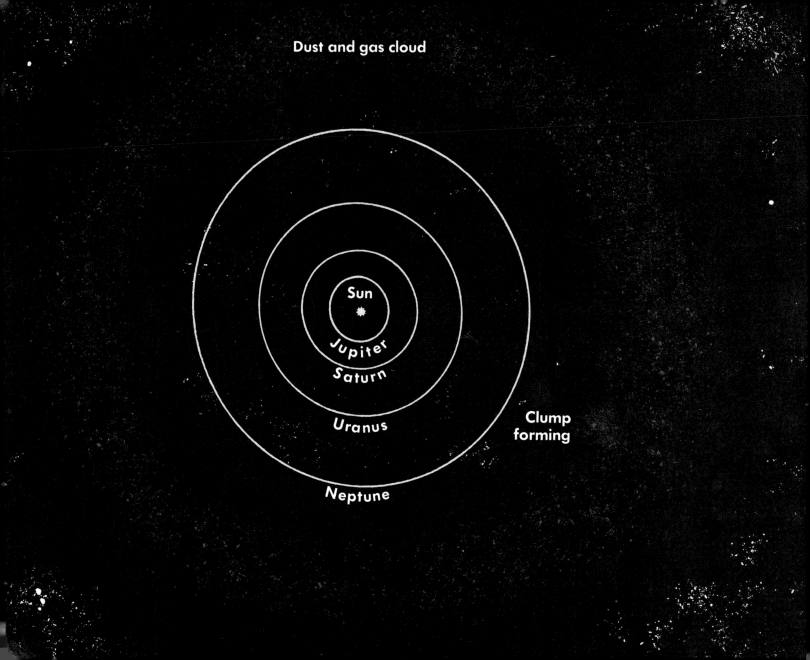

There are millions—maybe even billions—of comets in our solar system. New ones are probably forming all the time.

Way out beyond the sun and the planets there is a big cloud of dust and gases. It surrounds the solar system. Scientists believe that comets are formed from the dust and gases of this cloud.

No one knows exactly how comets are formed, but some scientists think it happens like this:

The particles of dust and gas are loose and far apart. All of them are moving. Once in a while, some of the particles collide and join together to make a clump. The clump collides with other particles, and so it grows larger.

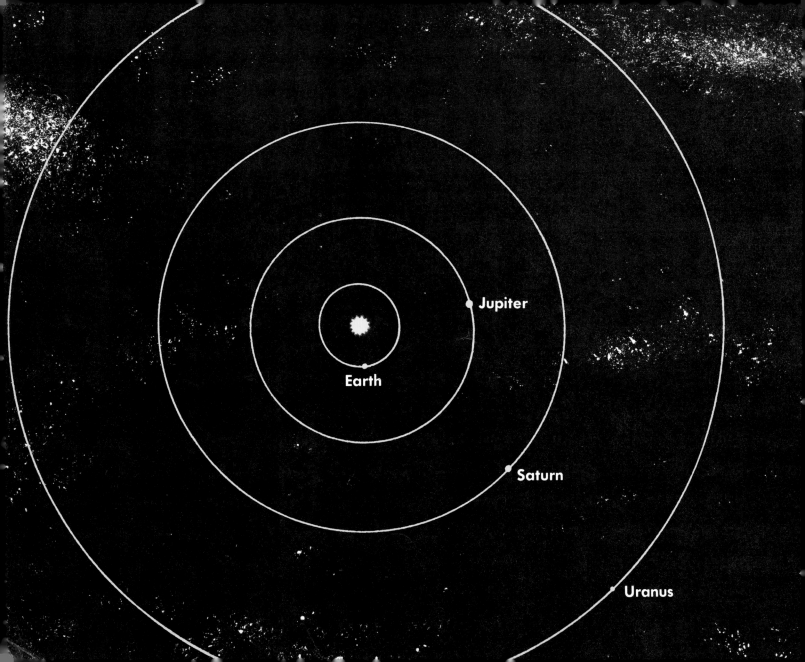

Neptune

The clump may be pulled out of the cloud by a star
as it passes by the solar system.
Its gravity pulls on the clump.
Jupiter also pulls on the clump. Jupiter is a
giant planet, and it has strong gravity.

Clump

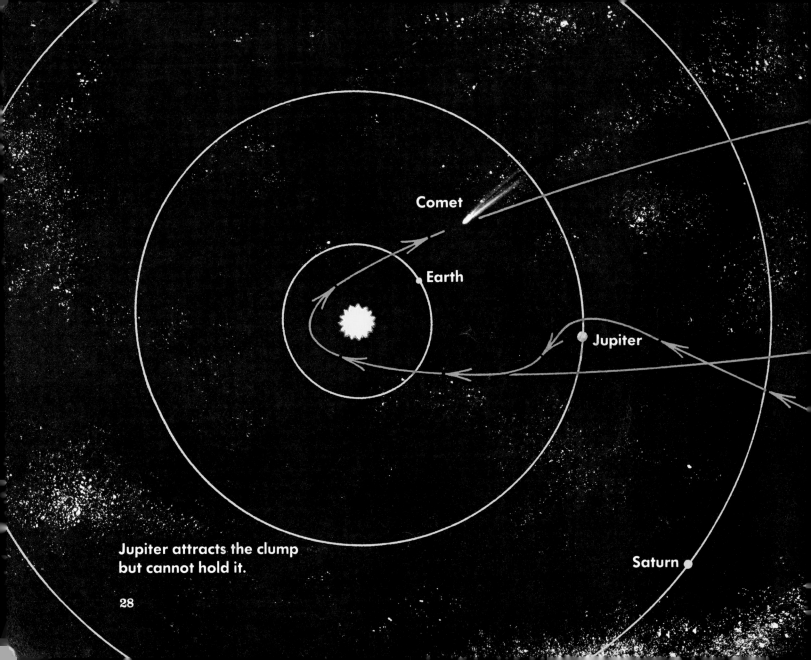

Comet

Earth

Jupiter

Saturn

Jupiter attracts the clump
but cannot hold it.

28

Neptune

Uranus

 Path of comet

 Path of clump

The clump is pulled into the solar system. It goes into orbit around the sun because of the sun's even stronger gravity. It has become a comet.

Each year astronomers discover new comets. Some of them are seen only once. They make one trip around the sun and then go way out into space. The sun's gravity cannot hold them.

Halley has been
losing dust for
thousands of years.
Even after Halley has
disappeared entirely its
dust will remain in the
solar system.

Other comets, like Halley, keep returning. They
have been captured by the sun. Halley's earliest visit
was probably 3000 years ago. It may keep returning
for another 3000 years.

But every time a comet goes around the sun, the comet loses part of itself. Gases and dust are pulled out of the comet. That's why Halley is now dimmer than it used to be. Next time it visits us, in 2062, it may be even dimmer. Each visit it may get dimmer and dimmer, until it finally disappears.

31

If you saw Halley in 1986, you can tell your children about it. You can tell them it was also seen by Edmund Halley, and by Julius Caesar long before Halley saw it.

Your children and grandchildren will see it in 2062. Perhaps you will see it too.

Between now and 2062 you may see many other comets. Some will be comets we already know about. Others will be new. They will be making their first journey around the sun.